Little Bear's Shapes

Little Bear's Shapes

JANE HISSEY

RED FOX

square circle triangle rectangle star semi-circle

square

square flag

cube   sphere   pyramid   cone   cuboid   cylinder

The toys are cutting out square windows.

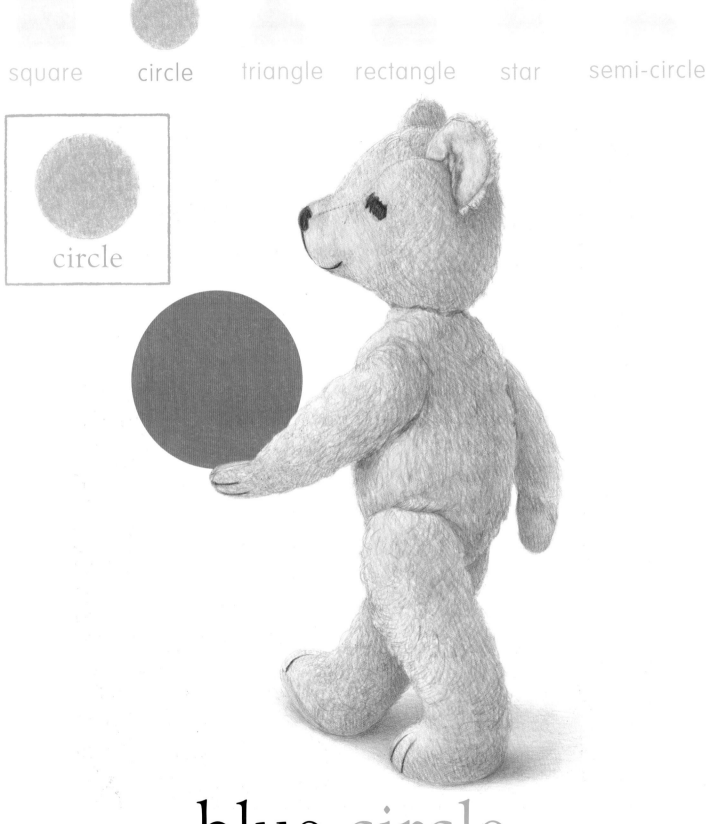

square circle triangle rectangle star semi-circle

circle

blue circle

Bruno's wooden hoop is a circle.

square circle **triangle** rectangle star semi-circle

triangle

red triangle

cube   sphere   pyramid   cone   cuboid   cylinder

Little Bear's dragon mask has triangles for teeth.

square circle triangle **rectangle** star semi-circle

rectangle

See-through rectangle

The bears are all holding paper rectangles.

square   circle   triangle   rectangle   star   semi-circle

star

paper star

cube   sphere   pyramid   cone   cuboid   cylinder

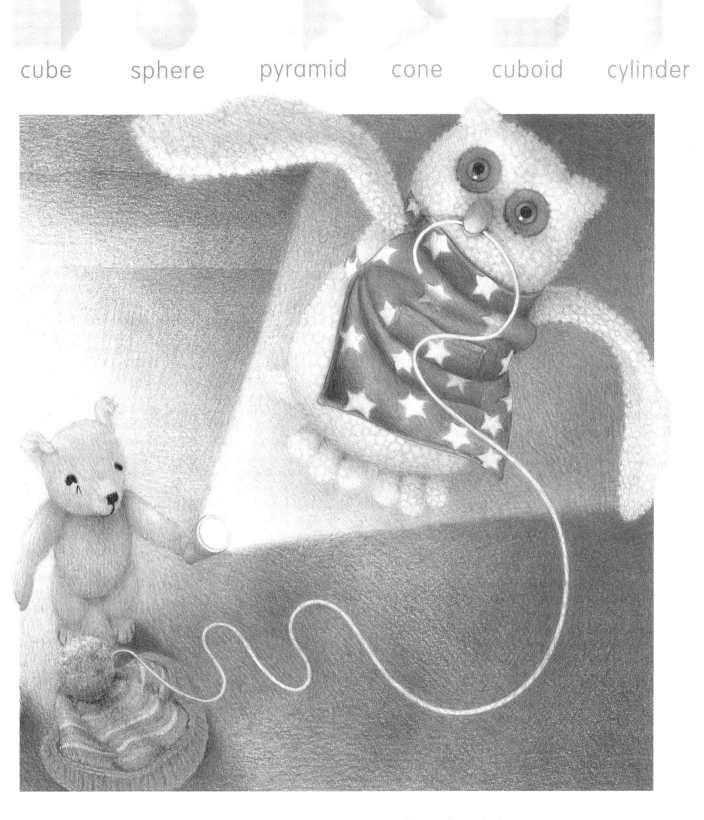

Hoot has stars on her apron.

semi-circle

biscuit semi-circles

Bramwell is pointing to a yellow semi-circle.

These are all two-dimensional –
2-D – shapes. They are flat.

These are all three-dimensional –
3-D – shapes. They are not flat.

square   circle   triangle   rectangle   star   semi-circle

cube

wooden cubes

cube sphere pyramid cone cuboid cylinder

Ruff's birthday cake is a cube.

square   circle   triangle   rectangle   star   semi-circle

sphere

glass sphere

The ball the toys have found is a sphere.

square   circle   triangle   rectangle   star   semi-circle

pyramid

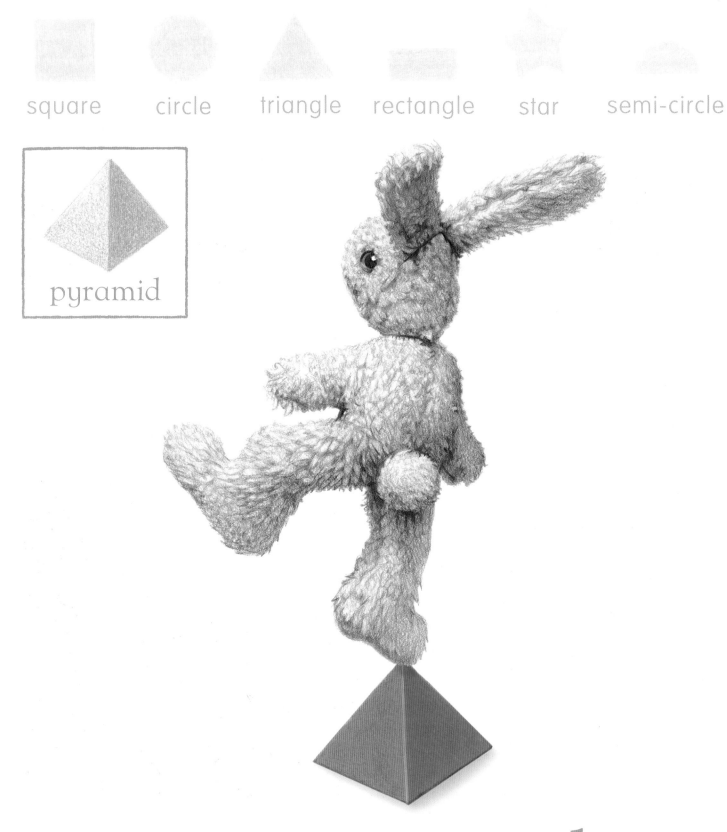

green pyramid

Camel is galloping past some pyramids.

square   circle   triangle   rectangle   star   semi-circle

cone

ice-cream cones

cube   sphere   pyramid   **cone**   cuboid   cylinder

Little Bear and Ruff have cone-shaped hats.

square circle triangle rectangle star semi-circle

cuboid

cuboid suitcase

Sarah Elizabeth's sewing box is a cuboid.

square   circle   triangle   rectangle   star   semi-circle

cylinder

wooden cylinder

cube   sphere   pyramid   cone   cuboid   cylinder

Bramwell's rolling pin is a cylinder.

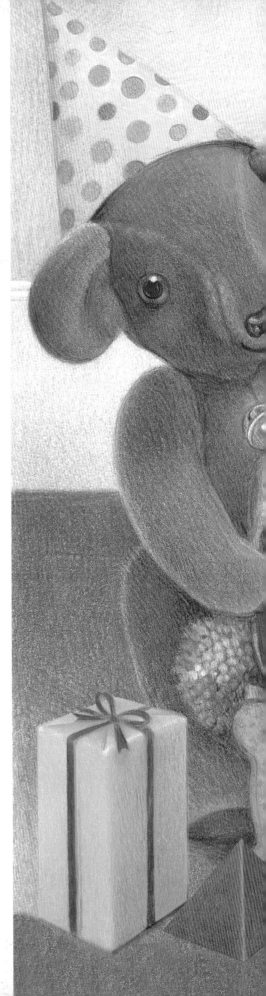

How many shapes
can you find?

For Susan and John

LITTLE BEAR'S SHAPES
A RED FOX BOOK 0 09 944748 7

First published in Great Britain by Hutchinson,
an imprint of Random House Children's Books

Hutchinson edition published 2003
Red Fox edition published 2004

1 3 5 7 9 10 8 6 4 2

Red Fox Books are published by Random House Children's Books,
61–63 Uxbridge Road, London W5 5SA,
a division of The Random House Group Ltd,
in Australia by Random House Australia (Pty) Ltd,
20 Alfred Street, Milsons Point, Sydney, NSW 2061, Australia,
in New Zealand by Random House New Zealand Ltd,
18 Poland Road, Glenfield, Auckland 10, New Zealand,
and in South Africa by Random House (Pty) Ltd,
Endulini, 5A Jubilee Road, Parktown 2193, South Africa

THE RANDOM HOUSE GROUP Limited Reg. No. 954009
www.kidsatrandomhouse.co.uk

A CIP catalogue record for this book is available from the British Library.

Colour reproductions by Dot Gradations Ltd, UK
Printed in Singapore